Workp

MW00877906

How to Survive and Thrive with a Bully Boss

By David Leads

Site: http://www.relationshipup.com

Books: http://www.relationshipupbooks.com

Your Free Gift

In 1938, 268 Harvard undergraduate men were followed for 75 years in what became one of the longest longitudinal studies of human development. Its purpose was to figure out what exactly contributed towards a good life.

Harvard Professor George Vaillant directed this study for more than three decades. Over and over again in his research he reiterated the power of relationships. In March 2008, he was interviewed and asked what he had learned from the study. His response –

> "That the only thing that really matters in life are your relationships to other people."

We believe your relationships are truly the most important thing in your life too. And in addition to the relationships you have with others, the relationship you have with yourself is also important. If you don't have a good relationship with yourself, it's hard to have good relationships with others. Everything we do at Relationship Up revolves around these two types of relationships you have – that with yourself and that with others.

The purpose of this book and all of our other publications is to help you improve your relationships so you can live a happier life. However, one thing that can easily get in the way of a good relationship is conflict.

Conflict between people happens all the time – and it's a major issue that disrupts relationships. Learning to prevent conflict and manage it when it arises is a skill you can learn that will improve your relationships across the board.

There are small tips, tactics, and strategies you can use to get better at keeping the peace between yourself and others. We compiled these in a book for you – *The 37 Best Ways to End Conflict in Your Relationships.*

In this book you'll learn the *what* and the *why* of each of the 37 ways to end a conflict. Even if you just implement one new way to end conflict you'll make lasting positive changes to the way you deal with other people.

As a way of saying *thank you* for your purchase, we're giving you this free book – exclusive to our readers.

Please visit our website to get your free gift.

The 37 Best Ways to End Conflict in Your Relationships

DAVID LEADS

What is Relationship Up?

There's so much information on the Internet about relationships, how to get along with people, and how to be a better person. Just doing a quick Google search on a personal problem you're currently having can leave you overwhelmed with the number of sources out there. We asked a lot of people where they went online for relationship help and advice. A lot of the responses we received indicated that people **didn't** use the Internet to find help with relationships. Instead they would go to their family, friends, clergy member, or spouse.

Why not look online for relationship advice? All the other information in the world is online, so why leave out relationships?

The response was – nothing out there is trustworthy. The sites people did frequent were *tabloid-like* in their presentation and information. Pretty much talking about sex 24/7 while ignoring a host of other common problems people have. Those sites seem to be more focused on clicks than on genuinely helping people. Also, people said that relationship problems are inherently unique, with each person facing a different problem in different individual circumstances. While this is true, there are principles and things people can do that can help them in any situation. Though our situations and life perspectives are always unique, others have experienced the same underlying issues before, and we can learn how others have done it in the past to increase our own wellbeing.

Relationship Up started in order to filter through all of this noise. We're interested in the principles that work, and we're even more interested in what to do and how to do it. We publish books on specific relationship issues with the intention that they are easy to understand, quick reads, and full of actionable and valuable information.

Everything we write about relates to issues between people, or issues you have with yourself. We hope that we can help people improve their relationships and thus add meaning to their lives.

We're just getting started so please leave a review for this book and let us know what you think, how we can improve, and how we can do better.

Visit us at http://www.relationshipup.com or email us at info@relationshipup.com

Table of Contents

Introduction

The workplace is where you spend a significant portion of your life. And, if you're lucky enough to be doing a job you love to do, it can also be one of your greatest sources of personal satisfaction and accomplishment. Yet, dealing with serious problems in the workplace can take all the joy out of your occupation. Beyond that, it can cause you physical, mental, social and financial harm.

How prevalent is workplace bullying? You might be surprised how many people it affects. The Workplace Bullying Institute offers the following statistics from its 2014 WBI U.S. Workplace Bullying Survey: 27% of workers are being bullied now or have been in the past. 72% of the American public is aware of specific bullying incidents in the workplace. 93% of those surveyed supported an anti-workplace-bullying law.[i]

When coworkers try to bully within a healthy corporation, there are safeguards in place to help their targets. But, what do you do if your boss is the bully? How can you possibly salvage your work life when the person in charge of you makes your daily work life a living nightmare? If this is the position you find yourself in right now, it might seem like you're stuck with living in misery at work or in poverty without a job.

Don't panic. You do have options, even when the bullying is at its worst. As you read this book, you can learn techniques for dealing with a bullying boss. But, before you start making a plan to counteract the bullying, you need to understand what workplace bullying is, how it applies to you, and how it affects every aspect of your life. Are you ready to stand up and take back control of your work life?

Chapter 1: Signs You're Being Bullied by Your Boss

What exactly is workplace bullying? Here's how the Washington Department of Labor defines it: "Workplace bullying refers to repeated, unreasonable actions of individuals (or a group) directed towards an employee (or a group of employees), which are intended to intimidate, degrade, humiliate or undermine; or which creates a risk to the health or safety of the employee(s). [ii]

The definition is pretty easy to understand in a general, theoretical way. Read it carefully to see how it applies to your situation. But, what does bullying actually look like in the workplace? Well, it's not nearly as neat and easy to recognize as you might think after reading this broad definition. Here are some ways a bully boss might attack you in the workplace.

Your Boss Verbally Abuses You

Most bully bosses won't actually cause you direct physical harm. For instance, your boss probably won't hit you over the head with a heavy piece of equipment or punch you in the jaw. If they do, you can press charges for assault. But, most bully bosses take the more subtle, and harder to litigate, route of abusing you verbally.

Your boss might verbally abuse you by telling stories about you that are designed to humiliate you. Or, they might call you derogatory names or put you down. Sometimes these negative statements are also combined with a harsh, mocking or angry tone of voice that makes you feel like you're being personally attacked. Another form of verbal abuse is the silent treatment or, in other words, treating you like you don't exist.

Make no mistake. The fact that the bully is "only" talking doesn't excuse this behavior. And, if you feel you deserve it, you need to understand your rights in the workplace better. Sure, you might expect your boss to point out your mistakes to help you do better, but they need to keep their tone of voice civil and their words respectful. The goal should be to help you do your work better and not to undermine you. No one deserves to be verbally abused, no matter how bad a job they're doing. And, chances are, you're already doing your job to the best of your ability given the lack of support you are dealing with.

The Bully Isolates You

Isolation is a sneaky way your boss might bully you. They might isolate you physically by putting you in an office far away from the others in your department. They might also isolate you by insisting that you take your breaks somewhere different from the others. One example would be telling you that you need to take your break at your desk to avoid wasting time while others are gathering in the break room. A bully boss might also separate you by making you take your break at a different time than others. For instance, they might tell you it's part of your job to clean up the break room, and that's why they're scheduling your break after the others go back to work.

Your boss might also isolate you from the work process by not including you in meetings where all the other members of your department are present. Your boss might be very sly in coming up with excuses for why it's happening, but the reality is that you're just as important a part of the team as others at the same level in your department, and you should be included.

The Bully Sabotages Your Work

Is your boss setting you up to fail? Sabotaging your work is a common method bully bosses use to undermine their target's confidence. Sometimes, it's not easy to recognize sabotage. When you're a team player and expect others to be, it's natural to think of what you can improve rather than to assume that the other person is playing with your mind. But, that's exactly what many bully bosses do.

Here's how Suzie's boss Dominique sabotaged her work:

Suzie was working as a teacher's assistant under head teacher Dominique in a daycare center. Dominique was supposed to guide Suzie as she helped prepare the classroom and the learning materials for the upcoming season. It was The Fall, and Dominique told Suzie to make construction paper leaves. Suzie asked if there were any particular colors to choose, and Dominique handed her a stack of brown paper. So, Suzie made brown leaves. Next, Dominique was arranging for parents to volunteer. She gave Suzie a list of parents to call and pointed to the top name – Jane Dixon – as the one Suzie should start with. Suzie did everything Dominique asked her to do and went home feeling that the day had gone fine.

The next day, when Suzie arrived at work, Dominique was standing at her desk, talking to the daycare CEO. She was showing the CEO those brown leaves. She said, "The leaves are so dark the kids won't be able to see their names when I write them on them. And she asked Jane Dixon to do a volunteer project with Jane in the hospital. I'm concerned that Suzie won't work out here."

Suzie felt confused and wondered if she had misunderstood Dominique's directions. And, that is exactly what Dominique wanted her to feel. With each passing day, Dominique gave her more difficult jobs to do along with instructions that she later denied. The final straw was when Dominique told Suzie to take a child into the restroom to check for bruises, saying that her parents were suspected of child abuse. When Suzie came out of the restroom, she saw the satisfied smile on Dominique's face. She suddenly knew it had been a setup to make Suzie herself look suspicious. Suzie walked out of the room and went straight to the daycare manager's office to defend herself before she could be attacked.

Suzie let the situation go way too far because she didn't recognize Dominique was maliciously targeting her for bullying. Because the CEO sided with Dominique, Suzie felt so helpless that she quit and spent several months sitting at home worrying about her future.

In this example, Suzie didn't really grasp what was happening to her until the bullying had escalated to dangerous levels. If your boss's instructions make you wonder whether they're setting you up to fail, don't wait to find out what might happen. Instead, use the techniques in this book to evaluate and address the bullying effectively before it causes you physical, emotional, financial or career damage.

The Bully Lies to Your Coworkers and to Upper Management About You

Sometimes the first signs of bullying you notice are lies your boss tells your coworkers or the main boss about you. In the previous example, Dominique misrepresented what happened at the school during prep week. Some bosses tell completely fabricated stories about their employee that relate to nothing that happened on the job. In fact, bully bosses usually choose lies that you can't prove or disprove. They make sure it's a case where it's your word against theirs. And, who do you think your coworkers are going to side with if they value their jobs?

The Bully Withholds Resources

The boss who withholds resources like overtime, time off, supplies, clients or budgeted funds from you is another one of those bullies who can hide behind apparent niceness to make your work life harder. This kind of bully boss will probably have very logical-sounding excuses for why others get the goodies and you don't. All along, what they really enjoy is controlling you.

The Bully Threatens You

Some bullies are not so subtle. They come right out and threaten you. They might threaten to get you fired or even to hurt you physically. Sometimes, these bullies try to pass their threats off as jokes to your coworkers and upper management. At the same time, they go to great lengths to let you know, in ways you can't prove, that they really are serious. Most people in this situation find it so hard to believe that a boss would do what the boss is threatening to do that they doubt their feelings that the boss is serious. This is how the bully succeeds in keeping you off balance and controlling you for their own amusement.

Most bully bosses use a combination of these tactics to make you feel insecure, confused and even fearful. Why would they want to do this? Bullies are motivated by a variety of factors, from upbringing to past experiences. All you really need to know about their motivation is that they do these things to control you.

Chapter 2: What Being Bullied Can Do to You

When you realize you're being bullied and turn to others for help, the response might go something like this: Work is hard. You have to be tougher. Quit whining and do your job. That's what work politics is like. You just have to get used to it. Nobody really likes their boss.

And the well-intentioned advice goes on and on. But when you analyze it, you realize that no one who gives you this kind of advice is really supporting your position. What none of these people seem to realize is that the bullying is causing you real harm and is likely to cause you even greater harm the longer you allow it to go on. Here are a few of the ways bullying can impact every part of your life.

It Causes Emotional Damage

Any style of workplace bullying is almost sure to result in emotional damage for you. You might become anxious or depressed as you try to maintain focus on your job despite interference from your bullying boss. At its least harmful, bullying can make you feel timid and insecure. At its most harmful, it can become so distressing or depressing that you take your own life. Do you find it hard to believe that bullying can result in suicide? If so, that's good. It means your bully hasn't broken you – at least not yet. If you're already starting to think about it, seek professional help immediately. This is serious business, and others have paid with their lives for not recognizing the emotional damage they were suffering because of their bullying boss.

Bullies can also exacerbate any mental weaknesses you might have or even cause you to develop them. When you're dealing with the slyest of bullies, reality can become a slippery thing. The person you are supposed to rely on to guide you in your work is presenting you with a distorted perspective that, deep down, you really know isn't true for you. Yet, they've undermined your confidence so much that you question your own intuition about what's really going on. When this goes on long enough, it can color your whole view of the workplace, and you can even become paranoid.

It Has Physical Effects

People who've been bullied in the workplace can suffer from any of a long list of physical ailments related to the stress of the situation. The Workplace Bullying Institute has done research to identify the most common physical problems of people who have been bullied at work. They include cardiovascular damage, negative neurological changes, gastrointestinal problems, impaired immune system and auto-immune disorders. To be even more specific, 60% of bullied workers developed high blood pressure, 21% developed fibromyalgia, 33% developed chronic fatigue syndrome, 10% became diabetic and 17% developed skin disorders.[iii]

The 2012 Workplace Bullying Health Impact Survey identified the most commonly reported physical effects of bullying as "anxiety (76%), loss of concentration (71%), disrupted sleep (71%), hyper vigilance symptoms (60%), and stress headaches (55%)."[iv]

It Can Cause You to Lose Your Job

Do you think you can stay on the job after you are targeted by a bullying boss? You might think you have what it takes, and you might be right. But, the chances are greater that you'll lose the job you once enjoyed. You'll be fired, transferred, laid off, demoted or voluntarily quit. This happens in over 3/4 of the cases of workplace bullying by a boss, according to a 2012 survey by the Workplace Bullying Institute.[v]

It Can Cause Problems at Future Jobs

If you assume that your problems will be over once you get away from your bully boss, you might be disappointed. Here are two important ways being bullied at one job can affect the next. First, once you've been bullied, you look at the workplace differently. Even if you get a job in a fantastic, cooperative work environment, you'll tend to look at your new boss with suspicion. You'll be a less joyous worker until you deal with the workplace trauma you've experienced. And, you'll likely find it hard to give the new job your all.

Second, the bully boss can pull strings to cause you trouble at a new job. Sometimes when you apply for a job, your prospective employer will have a conversation with your old bully boss. Is it legally correct? Of course not. But that doesn't mean it can't happen, especially if the two of them know each other. Some bosses have gone as far as to apply for management in a store where their target has moved. Of course, all of this is most likely to happen in small towns and other locations where people work and live in the same small area. But, even in a big city, a malicious boss can cause problems at the new place of employment.

Financial Troubles

Losing your job can lead to a world of financial hurt, especially if you aren't prepared. Statistics published on the FDIC site describe a situation where many Americans are on the brink of financial disaster even before they lose a job. According to these statistics, 43% of American households spend more than they bring in every year. 52% live from one paycheck to the next. 42% wouldn't be able to support themselves for 3 months if they were to lose their income temporarily.[vi] Bills go unpaid, utilities get shut off, there's not enough food in the house, or you might even become homeless.

Does the situation sound bleak? For many Americans it definitely is. And, if you're trying to survive at work despite being bullied by your boss, it's perfectly understandable if you're worried about your finances. Who wants to face that kind of financial adversity? No one.

Relationship Troubles

Keeping your relationships strong during times of workplace stress isn't an easy task. Family members often blame the target for allowing themselves to be bullied. Others simply don't want to know or hear about it. The balance can shift in a marriage because the bully's target feels so weak and ineffective at work. This can play out in two different ways. Either you want to reclaim your power by trying to control your spouse or your feeling of weakness takes over your marriage relationship too, and you give up all control. It takes an enormous effort and commitment to maintain a healthy, balanced marriage in the face of such a distressing situation.

Take an assessment of your life right now. Are you feeling emotionally different than before the bullying started? Have you noticed any new symptoms of physical illnesses or have chronic illnesses taken a turn for the worst? What about your finances? Are you prepared to do what you need to do to put the bullying behind you, even if it means spending some time looking for a new job? Now, think about your personal relationships. Do you feel more distant or at odds with your romantic partner? Are your friends and family supporting you in beneficial ways? When you have a clear picture of the damage your bully has created in your life, you can begin to understand how serious the problem is and get ready to wrap it up your own way.

Chapter 3: Why You're the Target of a Bully Boss

As you get a clearer picture of how your boss is bullying you, your first question might be "why me?" After all, you've done nothing to deserve this treatment. You're always more than willing to do your job to the best of your ability. You're not a slacker or a complainer. So, why is this happening to you instead of to someone else?

In most cases, certain types of people are targeted for bullying by a boss, and these people tend to respond to being bullied in the same ways. Here are some of the most common reasons a bullying boss might choose you as a target.

You Favor Cooperation Over Competition

Cooperation is beneficial to employers, right? It certainly can be if the employer prizes teamwork and getting the most productivity from each worker. But, bosses who are bullies tend to take advantage of people who aren't cutthroat competitors. They take it as a sign of weakness, not understanding or caring that employees can get more done by working together. When you prefer to cooperate rather than compete, you're more likely to unintentionally offer your bullying boss more opportunities to bully you. It happens because you're considerate of their needs and their feelings and put less importance on what you see as your own selfish wants. All the time you are thinking this, your bully boss is using your attitude to get more goodies for themselves and squeezing you out of the picture at work.

You Expected the Workplace to Be a Friendly Place

Before your boss began to bully you, your version of reality might have been that employment was enjoyable and people at work generally meant you no harm. Then, when the bullying started, you were taken totally off guard. This kind of dissonance between your expectations and your perceptions can be very unsettling and can make you feel extremely confused. The most likely result of being bullied after having such expectations is that you blame yourself for the situation. You might say to yourself, "The boss meant me no harm, so I must have done something to provoke them." You need to work on changing your thinking so you realize that the bullying boss is the problem and not you. If you can't make that shift on your own, it's time to seek outside counseling.

You Didn't Stand Up to the Bully Right Away

If your first reaction to being mistreated was to play nice and try to get along, you're not alone. Other targets have done the same thing. And, many people live by these ideals without ever being bullied by their boss or anyone else. Yet, once the bully picks on you, you essentially give them permission to abuse you if you don't put a stop to it right away. It might be too late now to worry about what you might or might not have done when the bullying started. And, don't punish yourself for making the wrong choice. You likely did it because you have high moral and ethical standards for yourself. It's nothing to dwell on now. But, in the future, remember that it's best to insist that you are treated well from the beginning. You can still be nice, you just need to be firm.

Upper Management Allows Bullying

Have you ever wondered why upper management at your company doesn't do something to help you deal with your bullying boss? It's possible your main bosses don't know what's going on. Your immediate boss isn't likely to expose their own bullying ways. So, if you haven't exposed the bully, chances are no one else has. But, what about when the bullying is blatant or it happens in front of upper management? How can you explain that? In many companies, upper management knows about the bullying and allows it to happen.

Why would someone responsible for the health of the company's bottom line allow bullying that undermines your productivity? First, you have to realize that upper management may not look at it that way. They might believe that the bullying will push you to do better. Or, your higher-level boss might be good buddies with the bully and doesn't want to upset or offend them. If the next level up from your boss is the company's owner, they might not be involved in daily operations. And, the truth is that some bosses just don't care.

Knowing why you were targeted probably won't relieve the situation. But, understanding that the bully didn't choose you as a target because you're a bad worker, unintelligent or soft can help you seize the power you need to deal with the bully in a way that benefits you.

Chapter 4: Dealing with Your Emotions

Bully bosses just love to play with your emotions. Many bully bosses pretend to be friendly part of the time, just so they can get your hopes up and squash them later. Controlling you that way makes them feel powerful and infinitely superior to you. Keep in mind that the bully wouldn't need to control you if they already felt powerful and superior. They would work to succeed in the business rather than focusing so much energy on you.

However, no matter what the bully does to you or why, you have emotions about it that you need to deal with. If at any time, you feel overwhelmed by your emotions or they prevent you from making choices you would ordinarily make, it's best to seek help from a professional counselor.

This chapter will help you understand your emotions well enough to decide if you need to start therapy. And, you'll get pointers on how to deal with your emotions on your own until you can get the help you need.

Avoid Self-Blame

Avoiding self-blame is hard when your boss is constantly pointing out your supposed mistakes. Yet, you'll decrease your power in the situation if you put thought and energy into blaming yourself for what happened. You're not only being unfair to yourself, but you're also magnifying your faults in your own mind. The bully's done that enough. They don't need your help with it.

Focus on the positive qualities you bring to the workplace and give yourself credit for the things you did right. If you catch yourself accepting the blame for the bullying, remind yourself that you didn't do anything to make your boss into a bully. They were that way when they first chose to single you out for bullying.

Deal with Your Anger

Therapists used to tell their clients to express all their anger and get it out. More recent studies show that when you dwell too much on expressing every angry thought and feeling, you turn up the intensity of your anger. In one study cited by the Association for Psychological Science, participants were told to pound nails into boards after becoming angry at people who insulted them. The participants' anger didn't go away at all. In fact, they showed even more anger towards those who called out the insults.[vii]

So, what are you supposed to do with your anger? The article mentioned in the previous paragraph also discusses how to express anger appropriately while applying problem-solving techniques. The message here is that you do need to be assertive in expressing not only what you feel, but also why and what you and the others involved need to do about it.

Overcome Hopelessness

To overcome hopelessness, you need to rediscover your strengths and the opportunities available to you. Your bullying boss has robbed you of your belief in a bright future. But, the picture your boss has painted for you is actually an ugly illusion. The truth is that, no matter how bleak the future looks right now, as long as you're still alive there's still hope.

It can be hard to convince yourself that there's something worth hoping for. You need time and possibly professional help to heal emotionally before you start reaching toward the future. But, you can start putting out feelers for job openings. Read help wanted ads and talk to people you know about potential openings. Also, you can take courses in your field to prepare yourself for a new job or to improve your work at your current job. Engaging with information about your career field can keep you focused on positive possibilities.

Check Excessive Optimism

Just as you need to guard against overly negative emotions, you also need to stay grounded in the reality of your situation enough not to give in to naïve optimism. Yes, there is much to be hopeful about. You're still alive. You've gotten at least one job in your life and you can get another.

At the same time, you might become excited when you hear of someone getting their boss fired for bullying or someone in the news winning a harassment case that sounds similar to yours. Of course news like this can give you more hope to keep fighting. But, if you get too excited, you can let down your guard and give your bully a chance to exploit and demean you further. Looking at the world through rosy glasses can make you less careful about the decisions you make or the things you say. Until you're out from under the bully's influence, you need to stay sharp and be aware of both negative and positive sides of your work issues.

Where to Turn for Help

Your company probably has a counselor on staff or provides company counseling from their preferred therapist. Upper management will present this option as a free or low-cost solution to your emotional distress. Whatever they say about it, don't accept counseling from a company or company-referred counselor. You need a counselor who isn't affiliated with your company in any way. Otherwise, you face the very real possibility that the counselor will side with your employer.

There are several ways you can find a counselor. You can go to the government funded community mental health center if your income is low enough. Or, you can ask your primary care physician for a referral. Another way is to ask someone you know who's been through therapy. Look for a counselor that specializes in workplace trauma, or at the least, has experience with treating PTSD. When you have your first appointment with the unbiased therapist of your choice, keep in mind that you can still look for a different counselor if you don't work well with this one. Use the first session to find out if the counselor is on your side and if your personalities are compatible. Then, if you stay with the counselor, you can work out all your emotional issues to prepare yourself for dealing with the bully boss.

Chapter 5: Document the Abuse

Being bullied can make you feel confused about what's really happening. But, you can satisfy yourself that you're looking at the situation accurately by starting a quest to document every incident in which your boss bullies you. Aside from getting in touch with the reality of bullying, documenting can give you something constructive to focus on, an especially important point if your boss is destroying your productivity at work. Another reason to document the bullying is that you can use the evidence in court or when you negotiate terms of employment or resignation with your employer. Finally, you can create a realistic analysis of how much the bully is costing your company, which you can possibly use to convince upper management or the owner to side with you.

What and How to Document

Keep records of coworker eyewitness testimony. You can ask a coworker who's seen a bullying incident to write a statement. Or you can just talk to them, having them tell what they saw, and make an audio or video recording. If it's legal in your state, you can make the recording without notifying the witness. And, if you're in one of these "unilateral consent" states, you might be able to record the bullying incident itself.

In addition, write your own account of each bullying incident as soon as you get a chance. When you write it down as soon as possible, you can capture specific details that might be important in court or in negotiations later on. Each day, place a time stamp on the documentation for that day. You can do this with certain software programs like OnLock. You can also create a PDF of any text file. This ensures that others can't change the document. It also provides a time stamp so you can prove when you gathered the evidence.

Figuring Company Costs of Bullying

An important part of your challenge as the target of a bully is to prove to your company how the bully is impacting the bottom line. Include as many of the costs as you can think of so your main employer will understand just how beneficial it will be to stop the bullying. Here are some items you can add to your calculations:

1) Costs of frequent turnover such as COBRA payments and unemployment payments, costs for advertising job openings and recruiting new employees, and other costs related to filling spots vacated by targets of the bully. The Workplace Bullying Institute suggests that using a figure of 1.5 times the yearly salary of each lost employee will give you a result that estimates these costs.[viii]

2) The loss of revenue generated by the former employee. If you were a sales person, for example, you can use a figure equal to your last year's sales totals.

3) The costs of absenteeism. Calculate these costs by figuring the amount you were paid for time off you took to escape the bullying.

4) The costs of presenteeism. These are difficult to calculate exactly, but you can estimate how much more you would have produced if you hadn't felt the need to come to work when you were sick for fear of losing your job. One suggested method is to use a figure that is one-half of your pay for the period you were present in body only because you came to work sick.

5) The costs of legal actions taken by the employee. If you know someone who's sued your company because of bullying, find out what the settlement or judgment amount was, and estimate the amount the company would have paid for legal assistance.

6) Workers comp and disability payments to lost employees.

Just as you learned in math class as a young student, always show your work. In other words, show the breakdown of the costs. This helps upper management see how you arrived at your figures. Don't exaggerate, but be sure to include all the costs the bully is costing the company. Tally up the total and include those figures on the document as well. When your documentation is complete, you'll be ready to go to your employer with your calculations.

Chapter 6: Fight or Run?

At some point, you have to make a decision as to whether to stay on the job and fight the bully or to leave the company. Base your decision on the physical, emotional and financial toll the bully is taking on you. Also, think objectively about how likely upper management is to listen to you. Here are some of the advantages and disadvantages of each position.

Advantages and Disadvantages of Staying and Fighting

If you succeed in ending the bullying, you'll get to keep a job you've enjoyed doing. You'll likely feel a sense of relief and become emotionally stronger as a result of claiming the power and overcoming the bullying situation. You won't have to go without a salary due to the loss of the job. You won't have to spend the money or energy to fight your bully in court if you can handle it internally.

The disadvantages of staying and fighting mostly come to you if you don't succeed in ending the bullying. You might eventually end up unemployed anyway, after you've lost the fight. During the time you continue working under the influence of the bully, you'll likely suffer additional physical and emotional damage. And, you'll find it harder to get new employment after you're beaten down more by your bully boss.

Here's an example of how one man benefitted from staying with his company and fighting the bullying.

Allen was a furniture salesman in a large furniture store. His supervisor was bullying him every day he went to the job. He decided to stay on and fight the bullying because he didn't want to lose his customer base. After Allen went to upper management at his company and presented his calculations of the cost of keeping his bullying boss on the payroll, his employer was so impressed with the figures that she started following the costs herself. She decided to fire Allen's boss and give Allen a raise to reward him for saving the company so much money. Allen got to keep his most valued customers along with a job he loved. In the end, he felt stronger and more satisfied with his job than ever before.

Advantages and Disadvantages of Leaving the Company

You might find it hard to justify leaving the company, but there are several distinct advantages to moving on.

First, you stop the emotional and physical damages your bully boss is causing you and start the healing process right away. Second, you can choose when you leave and look for a job before you leave your current job. Finally, if you leave on your own terms, you can still hold your head up high, knowing that you did the right thing for you and your family.

The disadvantages mostly show up if your exit experience is a negative one. If you get no satisfaction from the company and they side with your boss, you might become so discouraged that you find it hard to look for other work. You'll likely end up feeling defeated and find it hard to believe in yourself for a long time after you leave. And, your relationships might suffer because you chose to give up the job rather than stay and fight.

Here's an example of the advantages one woman found in leaving her job and moving on.

Jessica had been bullied by her boss for several months. She was beginning to notice in herself new symptoms of anxiety, and her doctor diagnosed her with high blood pressure. She decided that she'd be better off if she left as soon as possible. She started job hunting the same day she made this decision. In the meantime, she avoided her bully boss as much as possible. Within two weeks, she'd found a job at a new company where the atmosphere was more positive and cooperative. She was finally able to enjoy her work as she did when she first started in her career.

Jessica felt more personal power after refusing to participate in being bullied. She sought therapy to deal with the workplace trauma and quickly overcame her negative feelings. Feeling a renewed commitment to her health, she started taking her doctor's advice about how to keep her blood pressure under control. Soon, her readings were once again within the normal range and her doctor took her off the blood pressure medication he had prescribed.

Of course, not everyone has the positive experiences that Allen and Jessica had. However, if you follow the advice in this book, you can increase your chances of regaining your power in the same workplace or leaving on your own terms. Nothing is certain when you're dealing with a bullying boss, but you certainly can feel good about doing what you can to improve your work situation whichever way you choose.

Chapter 7: Gather Support

You've made your decision to stay or to move on to a new job. Now it's time to gather support for the decision you've made. It's time to reach out to people who can remind you of your worth and rebuild your confidence after it's been damaged by your bully boss. You've probably encountered positive people during your life that could help you feel more normal as you deal with your bully boss in your own way.

Can Coworkers Help You?

It might seem natural to go to your coworkers for help and support during your time of crisis. But, the truth is that coworkers usually feel they have more to gain and less to lose by siding with your boss. Remember that the coworker wants to keep their job just as you do, and they'll do anything they feel necessary to stay on the good side of the boss. Fear of retribution can be a powerful deterrent for coworkers who actually sympathize with you and wish they could help you. Because they have such a big personal investment in their job and tend to appease the bully boss, you're better off looking for help from outside sources.

Strengthen Existing Personal Relationships

Who are the most significant friends and family members in your life? Have your relationships suffered because of your preoccupation with your bullying boss? If so, now's the time to repair and improve those relationships. Spend more time with the important people in your life. Tell them what's going on at work, but don't dwell on it all the time when you're with them. Let them know you value them for who they are and appreciate their continued support.

Look Up Old Friends from Before You Had the Job with Your Bullying Boss

Working with a bullying boss can take up so much of your time and energy that it's easy to lose touch with the people who were good friends before the bullying started. Take some time now to get together with old friends. Don't limit yourself to friends who still live near you or who you've known as an adult. Look up your best friends from your youth. Take a weekend trip to spend time with friends living in different places. The more true friends you can gather, the more support you'll have as you deal with your bully boss.

Connect with People from Past Jobs

Have you had positive work experiences in the past? If so, you probably had close friendships with coworkers and/or employers you knew on those prior jobs. Although you're no longer working with them, you can rekindle those friendships. These people can be very important to you as you gear up for the battle ahead. And don't kid yourself. There will be a personal battle to fight whether you stay or leave. These people from prior jobs can help you recall the value you brought to your former employer. They can remind you of your positive qualities. And, even if you don't spend time talking about these issues with your former colleagues and supervisors, you'll feel better when you know there are people in the workforce who believe in you.

Chapter 8: Expose the Bully

Although confronting the bully is often ineffective, it's usually beneficial to expose the bully to others. Why? If you plan to stay, there is still a possibility that it can be a tool for eliminating the bullying. And, if you plan to leave, you need to let others know why you're quitting your job. This is how you maintain your dignity as you make your exit. Here's a step-by-step plan for letting others know what you've been experiencing.

1) Focus on Fact, Not Feelings

Your feelings are important to you, but they are not so important to others where you work. Spending a lot of time talking about your feelings makes you look weak and possibly even unstable. When you focus on the facts about the bullying, the problem ceases to be merely personal and becomes a workplace issue that others can relate to. You appear not only stronger but also sharper. And, by showing your intelligence and strength, you can stay or go with your head held high.

Before you approach anyone to talk about what's been going on, look through your documentation of the abuse. Refresh your memory about the details of each incident. Then, choose a few of the worst incidents to talk about with others. You might find it helpful to write out what happened in simple sentences that are direct and to the point. When the time comes, you don't have to recite these details verbatim. The exercise is not meant to provide a script but simply to remind you of the clear progression of how the incident unfolded so the details will come to you more easily and naturally.

2) Tell Coworkers What You've Experienced

Don't expect coworkers to help you eliminate the bullying for your sake. Each employee has their own agenda. As much as they might sympathize with you, they usually aren't willing to put your needs ahead of their own priority of getting along with the bully well enough to keep their own jobs. What you can expect, though, is that they'll be more alert to ways they themselves are being bullied. And, when they realize what the bully boss is capable of, they'll know why you're making the choices you're about to make. This may not help you deal with the bullying directly, but it can give you more confidence to follow through with your plans to end the bullying by appealing to upper management or leaving on your own terms.

Try to speak to coworkers in one-on-one situations. The reason is that your coworkers don't want others to know that they see themselves as vulnerable to the bullying. Herd mentality is always a factor when you're dealing with a group such as the group of workers in your department. If a coworker who is considered a leader by the group says unkind things with the others present, the whole group may turn against you. And, you certainly don't need that, especially when you're already dealing with a bullying boss. By speaking to coworkers individually, you make it easier for everyone to listen and judge for themselves. Also, remember that you're not going to your coworkers in an attempt to get them to put an end to the bullying. Your goal here is to state your case clearly and concisely so you can leave or stay with dignity and self-respect.

The good thing about herd mentality is that those in the know tend to influence others who haven't been told about the bullying. In a study at Leeds University, people were told to walk randomly in a specific area. A few leaders were secretly given more detailed instructions, but informed that they must not use words or gestures to let others know they had been given any instructions. In every case, the uninformed individuals followed the lead of those in the know. And, this phenomenon occurred when only 5% were given the detailed instructions.[ix] The other 95% followed the leaders of the group like sheep. How does this apply to your situation? If a few people decide that your bully boss is threatening their jobs, they will put pressure on the bully to behave better, and others will follow.

3) Tell Upper Management about the Issues

Within your company, upper management has the most power to help you. They offer you the greatest chance of working within the company to eliminate the bullying. At the same time, the people in upper management might be hard to convince. And that's why you need to bring along all your documentation, including the breakdown of what the bully is costing the company.

Ask to meet with someone higher up in the company than your boss. Send them an email or stop by their office to make this request. Meet with them at the time they specify and explain why you're there. Tell them about specific incidents, and then launch into your presentation about the costs to your company of allowing bullying to go on unchecked.

At the end of the meeting, ask the person you talked to if they can do anything for you. If you're satisfied with their response, let them know you appreciate their help and that you'll check back in if the problems continue. On the other hand, if they offer you little or no help, be ready to tell them what actions you're prepared to take such as quitting your job, asking for a transfer or even filing a lawsuit. Deal with them in a business-like way. That's what they understand and respond to, and that's what will offer you the greatest possibility of success.

Why HR Won't Help You

As you work to expose the bully to coworkers and upper management, you might be advised by various people to talk to the Human Resources Department of your company. After all, HR's job is to ensure that everyone in the workplace gets along and does their job, right? This is true only in a way that's based on what works for the company.

Tech Target defines Human Resources Management as "the people who work for the organization; human resource management is really employee management with an emphasis on those employees as assets of the business. In this context, employees are sometimes referred to as *human capital.* As with other business assets, the goal is to make effective use of employees, reducing risk and maximizing return on investment."[x]

This definition of HRM explains why you can't count on this department to look after your interests. Your needs are only important to them as they relate to the success of the company. But, won't you be a better worker if you aren't being abused by a bully boss? Yes, but here's the problem: your company probably has a lot more invested in your boss than it does in you. Therefore, your bully boss is the asset they most want to maximize.

Another thing to consider is the fact that, unless you're a member of a protected class of workers based on your gender, race, religion or disability, your issue is much less likely to end in successful litigation. While your company might be afraid of being accused of sexual harassment or unlawful discrimination, they have little to fear from an employee who doesn't fall into those categories.

Exposing the bully might or might not get you results. In any case, by the time you've told several people what's going on, you'll feel more self confident and ready to take whatever actions you need to end the bullying.

Chapter 9: Standing Up to the Bully

As mentioned in an earlier chapter, standing up to a bully boss is an ineffective way to end the bullying. So, why should you bother? There are two important reasons. First, this is another way to maintain or reclaim your dignity and self respect. Second, if you aren't leaving the job immediately, you'll need to ensure that you don't give the bully more opportunities to abuse you.

Demand to Be Heard

Bully bosses are great at demeaning, harassing and embarrassing the employees they decide to target. What they aren't so good at is listening to them. If your boss is bullying you, you can be sure that they are on a power trip they don't want to end. Bully bosses are known to avoid situations with their targets where they aren't in complete control.

So, what do you do if your boss ignores you? You can't expect to change them, but you can show care and kindness to yourself. Think of it this way: if someone you loved were attacked by this bully, would you stand idly by and watch them suffer? Probably not. Instead, you'd confront the bully and let them know what they're doing is wrong. And, standing up for yourself is really no different in this regard from standing up for those you love. You don't want your loved ones to hurt, and there's no reason to let yourself be hurt either. So, demand that your bully boss listens to you. Demand by using direct language and by refusing to go away unheard.

Tell the Bully You Won't Accept Their Bad Behavior

Your emotional and physical health suffer more and more the longer you put up with the bullying. You might not be able to end it, but you can make it clear that you aren't going to go along with it. At the moment when your bullying boss attacks you, whether they attack subtly or obviously, let them know you're not going to accept the negative labels their bullying places on you.

Approach the bully in an assertive way that's neither intimidating nor compliant. Use a businesslike approach. Set aside your emotions for now and stay in a more logical mode. Speak in short, succinct sentences that describe what the bully is doing wrong and how you expect to be treated.

Clear Up Confusion about Work Duties

Bullying bosses just love to keep you guessing. They tend to give confusing or conflicting instructions and work assignments. The more they can muddy the waters and make you feel insecure about doing your job, the easier it is for them to control you. And guess what. That's exactly what they want.

So, it's up to you to clear up the confusion. When your boss gives you instructions that don't make sense or that conflict with earlier instructions, repeat back what they just said. Put it more clearly and say it in as few words as you can. Then, ask "is that what you want?"

Clear up these confusing instructions where other coworkers are ready witnesses.

Here's how Pete stood up to his bully boss by clearing up confusing instructions.

In Pete's job as a playground installer, he had to deal with a bully boss named Jack. Jack seemed to enjoy keeping Pete off kilter by frequently changing Pete's job duties. Before Jack came to the company, the routine had been for the supervisor to order the tools the installers would need for each job. The supervisor also served as a liaison between the customer and the company. The installers were required to be at the job site on time and do all the work of putting in the playground.

But, things didn't work so smoothly after Pete's former supervisor retired and Jack took over. One day, Pete went into Jack's office to get the specialty tools for the day. When he saw that there were no new tools, he asked Jack if he was looking in the wrong place for them. Jack told him, "It's not my job to get your tools. You need to take care of that yourself."

Pete was puzzled. He knew he couldn't order the tools because he didn't have access to company funds. Yet, when he tried to point that out, Jack told him that it was his (Pete's) responsibility to provide his own tools. Pete knew that many laborers in other types of companies do provide their own tools, but he had never heard of that being a requirement at his own job.

The whole conversation didn't make sense to Pete, because he felt that it would take a major policy change to add requirements like that. He was aware of no such changes. So, he decided that rather than stressing over what was true or not true, he would confront his bully directly and in open.

Pete knew that the owner of the playground company always stopped in at the installation office after the workers had arrived for the day and before going into his private office. So, Pete waited for his coworkers and the owner to arrive. When his employer stepped in, Pete said to Jack, "You want me to buy my own specialty tools for each playground. Do I understand that right?"

When the business owner heard this, he said, "Jack, did you tell him this?"

Jack said, "No, I don't know where he got that."

Pete then asked the employer, "So, you don't want me to buy my own specialty tools?"

The owner told him, "No. I think you misunderstood."

In Jack's case, the bullying didn't stop, just as it usually doesn't stop this easily. However, he did settle this one question. Then, when Jack demanded that Pete talk to a customer and work out a solution to an issue with the equipment that had been installed, Pete used this same method to clear up the confusion and avoid taking on the liaison duties that were rightfully Jack's. Clearing up confusion isn't a permanent solution, but it does make your work life more bearable in the meantime.

Chapter 10: Planning Your Exit Strategy

You might not want to leave a company because of being bullied, especially if you've been there for many years. And, if you just walk out the door with no preparation, leaving can seem like a personal failure. Also, you can make your work life easier by thinking about what you'll do if you decide to move on to another company. Planning a strong exit strategy will make things easier whether you stay or go.

Why You Need an Exit Strategy

Before you start working on your exit strategy, take a few moments to consider why what you're about to do is so important. First, your bully's abuse will seem less threatening to you if you know there are alternatives. Having a plan in place in case you need it will give you more confidence to do whatever you decide to do. Finally, if you do decide to leave, you'll be prepared to leave on your own terms. And, don't worry that planning an exit strategy is disloyal to your company. Karen Geier of Workopolis.com suggests that everyone should plan an exit strategy as soon as they start a job.[xi] Consider it as a normal part of being successful in the job market.

Get Positive Recommendation Letters

Start getting ready for future employment any time after you start a job by gathering recommendation letters. Ideally, you can ask people for them at times when you've just completed a project or earned an achievement. Get the letters from coworkers, other management besides your bully boss, vendors or clients who you've helped.

Here's how Lisa collected a handful of recommendation letters.

Lisa is a supervisor for retail salespeople in the kitchenware department of a large department store. Frank, her boss, is the department manager. He's been sabotaging her work and starting rumors about her. Frank has told her that the store manager is considering firing her. She doesn't know whether this is true, but she's starting to worry that even if he doesn't fire her, she'll become so stressed she'll have to quit. So, she's decided to be proactive and start preparing for a possible job change. She started by getting some recommendation letters.

Lisa had recently talked to Ella, a customer who works as a wedding planner. Lisa worked with the promotions department to arrange a group discount for Ella's clients. Ella was pleased with the arrangement and praised Lisa for setting it up. Frieda, in the promotions department, also told Lisa she was an asset to the company. And, John, the vendor who sells the kitchenware to the store, thanked her for increasing his sales.

Lisa got recommendations from Ella, Frieda and John the week after she realized the bullying was a major problem for her. She called Ella and requested a letter, which Ella gladly wrote for her. When she asked Frieda to write her a recommendation letter, Frieda told her that she'd already expressed her thanks to Frank, but that she'd be happy to write up a letter. John said he wished he could write her a letter, but he didn't have enough time in his office since he was usually out making sales calls. But, he gave her a business card and told her he would sign a letter if she would write it, which, of course, she did. From this one positive experience, Lisa gained three recommendation letters without trying to get one from her bully boss.

Warn Management of the Consequences of Giving a Bad Reference

Many job seekers believe that the only things your boss is allowed to tell prospective employers who call them for work history is that you worked for the employer and the dates you were employed there. However, there actually is no such clear cut law on the subject. So, you need to be aware that your boss can legally say anything they want about you.

However, if your boss tells intentional and malicious lies when asked for a reference, there may be something you can do legally. According to NOLO, there are several legal requirements you must meet to prove defamation of character. First, your boss must have made a statement that is malicious and false. They must have made it to or in front of a third party, which is known as publishing it. It must have injured you in some way. Losing the opportunity to get a job is the type of injury you'll most likely suffer. Finally, the statement must be made in an unprivileged setting. For example, if your boss makes the statement in court, they won't be punished because court testimony is privileged speech. However, if your boss says it to a prospective employer, that speech is unprivileged and you can sue for defamation of character.[xii]

If your employer is spreading false information about you, it's best to consult a lawyer. Before you even leave, though, you can make sure your boss knows about cases in which a former boss was on the losing end of a defamation lawsuit. You'll have to do some research to come up with examples. Also, you'll want to let them know subtly so you aren't provoking your boss to fire you immediately.

Find a Professional Reference Checker

Professional reference checkers call your former boss and ask for them for a reference. The way they word the request suggests, but doesn't say outright, that they're a prospective employer considering whether to hire you. Reputable reference checking companies keep detailed records of these calls and may record them. If your boss gives a negative reference that you don't deserve, you can use these records and recordings in court to prove defamation of character or, if you're a member of a protected class of workers, you can prove discrimination. Don't sign up for a reference-checking service while you're still employed. But, knowing who to call when and if the time comes is an important part of your exit strategy. By the way, sometimes you can avoid the problem of getting a negative reference from your boss by requesting that your employer not speak to your former employer.

Plan to Skip the Exit Interview

Do you dread going through an exit interview if you are fired or quit? Such a fear can increase your stress and sidetrack you from doing your current job to the best of your ability. The best way to counter it is to plan ahead to skip the exit interview. Remember that the exit interview is really for the company and not to benefit you.

Look for a lawyer who can write and send a formal letter to your employer. The letter explains to your employer that you're not going to attend the exit interview. It demands payment for work completed and spells out other legal rights. Knowing ahead of time who you'll call can help you avoid panicking when you're told you have to come in and talk to management before you can get your final check.

Prepare for a possible job search by soliciting positive references, finding a reference checking service you can count on, and letting your boss know about the legal consequences of telling malicious lies. Of course, when the time comes, you still need to use networking and resume building to prepare for a job change just as you would any time you're looking for work. Keep working on the exit strategy as long as you continue to work under your bully boss. You'll need it if you move on, and it'll give you self-confidence as long as you stay.

Chapter 11: Should You Sue Your Employer?

You've been wronged by your bully boss and by your employer for allowing the bullying to continue. You have probably suffered emotionally and physically. It stands to reason that you should have some legal recourse for dealing with the matter. And in fact, you do have legal options. However, before you decide to file a lawsuit, you need to consider it carefully.

Advantages and Disadvantages of Filing a Lawsuit

Getting Payback

If justice is important to you, filing a lawsuit might represent for you a means of getting what's rightfully yours. If you win, you might feel satisfied that the employer eventually did right by you, even if they did have to be forced to do it. If you lose, at least you'll have tried. But the result is often very different from this. According to the Workplace Bullying Institute, winning a lawsuit against a former employer because of bullying won't necessarily satisfy you. In fact, the WBI further explains that clients who have won as much as $1,000,000 or more still don't feel vindicated. The problem is that the bully is still free to bully, regardless of what the company pays you.[xiii]

Punishing Your Employer

You may be so angry after you realize the depth of the bullying that you want your employer to be punished. You want them to suffer as much as they've allowed you to suffer. There's nothing wrong with having those feelings, but filing a lawsuit may not be the best way to deal with the hurt.

Face it: there are very few protections in place for workers who aren't members of one of the classes protected by discrimination laws. In most states, employment is at will, so your employer is legally allowed to fire you for nearly any cause. So, if your bully boss fired you as a means of controlling you, they're probably within legal rights to do so.

Protecting Yourself against Future Bullying

You might believe that once you've sued an employer, you've sent the message to future employers that you won't allow yourself to be abused. The problem with that is that employers don't usually look at it that way. Instead, when they know you've sued for bullying, they see you as a risky investment and choose not to hire you.

The employer is very likely to retaliate after you've filed a lawsuit. While it's true that retaliation for a formal complaint is illegal, it's very hard to enforce. And, most employers retaliate in ways that are very hard to prove. And depositions can be so brutal that many people who've been targeted by bullies describe it as akin to intellectual rape. Add to that the trauma of reliving every moment of the bullying while testifying in court.

Chances are you'll protect yourself less by filing a lawsuit than by moving on with your life.

Closure

A lot has been said in popular psychology magazines and blogs about the importance of closure. Merriam-Webster.com gives two definitions of closure that might apply here. The first is that closure is "a feeling that something has been completed or a problem has been solved," and the second says that it is "a feeling that a bad experience, such as a divorce or death of a family member, has ended and that you can start to live again in a calm and normal way."[xiv]

If you're looking to court as a way to complete something or solve the problem of being bullied, you might get closure, but it'll be delayed for a long time as the court moves slowly toward a conclusion. If you're looking for a feeling that the bad experience is over, dwelling in it for those months or years won't help you. The best way to get closure if it doesn't come naturally is to seek therapy instead of a legal recourse.

Financial Gain

When you read that $1,000,000 figure earlier, or if you've heard of similar settlements, you might look at a lawsuit as a way to increase your financial security. You might imagine going on an expensive vacation to relax after the court case is settled. Or, maybe you see yourself contributing to your favorite charity with some of the extra funds. It would be nice if all this were possible, and in a few rare cases, it is. However, it's more likely you'll get a much smaller settlement. In fact, you'll be lucky if the settlement nets you very much at all after you pay the legal costs.

<u>Telling Your Story</u>

It's natural to want to tell others when someone wrongs you. You're not just getting it off your chest; you're also warning others so the same thing doesn't happen to them. You might imagine telling everyone you can about how you were mistreated. However, a lawsuit might not be the best way to do that. Why? It's because you'll probably have to agree not to talk about the settlement if you do get one. Your best hope to tell your story is to get a lawyer who can negotiate a gag order that only prohibits you from revealing the amount of the settlement. Then, you can say whatever you want about how the bully treated you and how little help you got from the employer.

How to Choose a Lawyer If You Sue

If you decide that the advantages outweigh the disadvantages, you need to find the best attorney to represent you in your workplace bullying case. There are no lawyers who specialize in workplace bullying because there are no specific laws to address it.

When you're interviewing lawyers, ask about their workload. If they're too busy to help you, you might not get the attention you need. On the other hand, if the lawyer has little to no workload, you need to do some research to find out why.

The best lawyer for you is one that represents mostly plaintiffs who are usually individuals rather than large companies. And, no matter who you interview, ask them if they've ever represented the employer or any of the upper management of the company you're suing.

Another consideration is how you're going to pay for the lawyer's services. If you don't have enough money to pay your lawyer, you might find one that'll do it on contingency. But, since there's a high risk of losing the case or winning a very minimal amount, you'll probably have to pay the lawyer in advance with a retainer.

What to Expect During the Lawsuit

The first thing to know is that most lawsuits over workplace bullying take years to resolve. During this time, you won't be able to put the past completely in the past. You'll constantly be reminded of the details and feelings surrounding this difficult part of your life. When the case does end, you'll probably get only a small settlement if you get one at all.

Another thing you need to know is that any coworkers from the company where you had a bullying boss are unlikely to stand behind you in court. They may be very sincere in wishing they could help you. The truth is that they know their jobs are on the line if they go against the company where they work.

Your bully boss will get a chance to take the stand and assault your character without fear of legal consequences. Remember that speech in court proceedings is protected speech. Your bully boss can say whatever they want about you. Your employer wants to protect his interests, so they'll come down on the side of the bully boss.

However, if you understand the difficulties associated with taking legal actions against a bully boss, you might still decide that it's worth the fight.

One of the main reasons many targeted workers choose to fight the legal battle is that they understand the impact they can make on the legal system of your country. Your case might not mean much by itself, but the more people that hold employers responsible for bullying in the workplace, the more the legal system will change to accommodate those needs. Your case might be a small drop in the bucket, but the cumulative effect of many bullied employees seeking justice will likely be a change in current laws and legal practices. You can make a difference. If that's important enough to you, you'll have the commitment you need to see the legal battle to its best conclusion.

Chapter 12: Healing from the Bullying

Once you end the bullying, you can concentrate on moving on with your life. It won't be easy. You'll need to stay connected with that support network you gathered for the fight and call on them as you rebuild your confidence and your life. And, you'll need to look for resources in your community to help you overcome the damage the bullying has caused you and your family.

Don't Push Yourself to Feel All Better Overnight

Your bully boss put you through emotional torture and likely damaged your health as well. Your relationships and your finances have also been negatively affected. So, it's not surprising that you feel emotionally drained or depressed. This emotional state didn't come about overnight. It took months or possibly years of being bullied to bring you to this emotional level. So, don't expect the feelings to go away immediately. Maybe your current job situation is enjoyable. Perhaps you've even filed a lawsuit over the bullying and won. It doesn't change your emotions immediately. Don't push yourself to feel better overnight. Embrace the positive, certainly, but also be kind to yourself in this difficult time.

Deal with the Workplace Trauma

Workplace trauma is a form of PTSD (post-traumatic stress disorder). When the work environment is unpredictable and you're dealing with a malicious, bullying boss, work can become emotionally similar to a war zone. You might not fear for your life, but you do fear for your livelihood.

The best way to deal with workplace trauma is to go into therapy. Choose a therapist who has a Master's in counseling or a PhD in psychology. Therapists who specialize in PTSD and trauma tend to be well-equipped for helping targets of workplace bullying. If you don't find such a therapist, choose one that specializes in the treatment of anxiety, domestic violence or who has certification in an anxiety-reduction technique called EMDR.

The first time you talk to the counselor or therapist, ask questions about their view of workplace bullying. Pay attention to their responses to your story and notice where they put the blame for the incidents. If they put the blame on you or on your childhood, they won't be able to help you deal with this very real, adult problem that your bully boss initiated.

Rethink Personal Standards

Most targets of workplace bullies have high moral and ethical standards. They tend to expect themselves to be perfect to meet some lofty ideal of the way a worker should behave. This is one reason targets often let bullying go on too long – they put the blame on themselves for not being the best worker in the company.

It's good to have high standards, but you need to temper them with some kindness for yourself. No one is suggesting that you become a slacker or that you stoop to the level of your bully. But, what you can do is stop being so hard on yourself when you don't meet your own expectations.

Spend Fun Time with Family and Friends

As you're dealing with the aftermath of workplace bullying, you need to spend some time enjoying your family and friends at times when you aren't talking about the workplace trauma. Certainly, you'll need to discuss the bullying issues during therapy. And, you'll need to deal with the practical issues such as getting a new job and resolving financial problems. You also may need to discuss the workplace issues as you repair relationships that suffered because of the bullying.

Yet, you need to get away from the problems sometimes. Getting away from the drama for a while will do you more good than dwelling on it constantly can ever do. Find time to enjoy weekend getaways with your significant other, going out with friends, and going to family gatherings.

Live, laugh and love.

Your life may seem to be all about being bullying right now, but that really isn't all it is. Look over your life for the good in it. Think about what you like in your life and what you want to build on. There is life after being the target of a bullying boss. All you have to do is reach out and claim it!

Conclusion

Workplace bullying is a very real problem. Now that you can recognize bullying in all its forms, you can take the next steps to deal with it, eliminate it from your life and move on. The process won't be easy, and it might take a long time. Don't let the struggle define you. Instead, when you think of the bullying, remember your courage, intelligence and inner strength in dealing with the problem. Being bullied doesn't make you a failure. When you work to overcome the effects of being bullied, you can honestly consider yourself a true success.

What you need to remember is that you still have good times ahead. Starting today, move towards living your life the way you want to live it. You can put this painful chapter of your life in the past. And, when you do it successfully, your life is going to be fuller, happier and more meaningful.

Now is the time to make a commitment to yourself to demand fair treatment at work. It's not only what you need. It's what you truly deserve.

Stay Connected

Thanks for reading this book. We hope you found this information helpful and actionable.

You can learn more about ways to improve your relationships from our other books on Amazon, and from our website.

Also, we frequently run special promotions where books in our catalogue are FREE or highly discounted (think $0.99) on Amazon.

We release 1-2 books per month right now – and friends on our list are instantly notified when we make these books free for a few days.

All of our deals are publicized exclusively via our email list.

Join now, and you'll instantly be notified when our freebies happen. Also, you'll get a free copy of our book *The 37 Best Ways to End Conflict in Your Relationships.*

Please visit our website to get on our mailing list!

Thank You

Before we part ways for now, we just want to say thank you for purchasing this book and a big congratulations to you for reading it all the way to the end!

There are tons of books out there on relationships, and you decided on this one, and we appreciate it.

If you have any questions, comments, or concerns, you can send an email to us at info@relationshipup.com or visit us on the web. We're always looking to make our books better – so we appreciate ALL feedback!

We'd like to ask for a favor right now – Please take 1 minute and 36 seconds (exactly!) and leave a review for this book on Amazon. Reviews help other people find our books and they help us understand what you liked and what you didn't like about the book – and we want to know what's on your mind so we can do better!

Thank you and all the best to you!

Sources

[i] 2014 U.S. Workplace Bullying Survey. Gary Namie, PhD, Research Director, Assistance from Daniel Christensen & David Phillips © 2014, Workplace Bullying Institute http://www.workplacebullying.org/wbiresearch/wbi-2014-us-survey/

[ii] "Workplace Bullying and Disruptive Behavior: What Everyone Need to Know." Safety and Health Assessment and Research for Prevention (SHARP). Washington State Department of Labor & Industries. April 2011. http://www.lni.wa.gov/safety/research/files/bullying.pdf

[iii] "Stress Related Health Impairment." Workplace Bullying Institute http://www.workplacebullying.org/individuals/impact/physical-health-harm/

[iv] " WBI Survey: Workplace Bullying Health Impact." Workplace Bullying Institute. 2012. http://www.workplacebullying.org/2012/08/09/2012-d

[v] "WBI Study: Attempts to Stop Bullying at Work by Targeted Workers Ineffective." 2012. http://www.workplacebullying.org/2012/04/20/effectiveness/

[vi] Financial Home and Help Organization. http://www.foreclosurehelpandhope.org/

[vii] "Myth #30: It's Better to Express Anger to Others than to Hold It In." Association for Psychological Science. http://www.psychologicalscience.org/media/myths/myth_30.cfm

[viii] "Estimating the Costs of Bullying." The Workplace Bullying Institute. http://www.workplacebullying.org/individuals/solutions/costs/

[ix] Nauert, R. (2008). "Herd" Mentality Explained. *Psych Central*. Retrieved on November 5, 2014, from http://psychcentral.com/news/2008/02/15/herd-mentality-explained/1922.html

[x] "Human Resource Management (HRM)." TechTarget: Essential

Guide. http://searchcio.techtarget.com/definition/human-resource-management-HRM

xi "Exit Strategy: The Smart Way to Leave Your Job." Workopolis.com, Karen Geier, April 10, 2014.
http://www.workopolis.com/content/advice/article/exit-strategy-the-smart-way-to-leave-your-job/

xii "Defamation Law Made Simple." NOLO.
http://www.nolo.com/legal-encyclopedia/defamation-law-made-simple-29718.html

xiii "Finding a Lawyer." The Workplace Bullying Institute.
http://www.workplacebullying.org/individuals/solutions/finding-a-lawyer/

xiv "Closure." Merriam-webster.com. http://www.merriam-webster.com/dictionary/closure

CPSIA information can be obtained
at www.ICGtesting.com
Printed in the USA
LVOW13s1155261217
560817LV00025B/1307/P